An interview with

Jacqueline Wilson

Other authors
in the series:

Enid Blyton, Theresa Breslin,
Gillian Cross, Anne Fine, Jamila Gavin,
Michelle Magorian, Michael Morpurgo,
Jenny Nimmo, J.K. Rowling

Joanna Carey is an author and illustrator in her own right.
She is a former children's books editor of *The Guardian*,
and still contributes. She is also a regular reviewer for the
Times Educational Supplement. Joanna also interviewed
Michael Morpurgo for this series.

Published in Great Britain 2000 by Mammoth.
This edition published in 2002 by Egmont Books Limited,
239 Kensington High Street, London W8 6SA.

Interview questions, design and typesetting © 2000
Egmont Children's Books
Interview answers © 2000 Jacqueline Wilson
Jacqueline's Books © 2000 Joanna Carey
The Bad Sister © 1998 Jacqueline Wilson

ISBN 1 4052 0055 3

Printed and bound in Great Britain by Cox and Wyman Ltd, Reading, Berks.

Contents

Foreword

Since 2000, when I originally interviewed Jacky Wilson, there have been some exciting developments. Two of her books, *Double Act* and *The Story of Tracy Beaker*, have been adapted for television and the schools television will be showing two documentaries about Jacky and her work.

One major change in her life is the fact that the ancient Olivetti manual typewriter that she has relied on for so many years has at last been replaced by a computer. But, even though she's now the proud owner of a beautiful turquoise (i.Book) laptop, there are times when her total involvement with whatever story is underway means that on short train journeys, for example, there really is no substitute for the trusty old notebook and pencil.

Jacky continues to look into the lives of ordinary children, as ever addressing difficult, often complex themes with great simplicity and immediacy by telling the story from the point of view of the child. Two of her recent books, *Vicky Angel* and *The Cat Mummy*, explore, from two very different angles, children's attitudes to death and her newest title, *Dustbin Baby*, tells the irresistible story of an adopted child desperate to find out the truth about her origins. 'I know that in early adolescence family misunderstandings can often cause children to fantasize about having been adopted, or handed to the wrong parents at birth,' she says, 'but this story was inspired by newspaper and TV reports of abandoned babies and orphanages . . . I wanted to write a positive story around the fact that however difficult it might be knowing nothing about your past, the important thing is to look not at what you *haven't* got, but what you *have* got – and only then is it possible to begin to make sense of your life.'

Jacky knows her audience inside out, she loves to talk to her readers and she's very generous with her time. She makes a huge number of school visits and personal appearances – in fact, of all our current children's writers she is probably one of the most accessible. But she does admit to worrying about the amount of time she spends travelling. 'I make so many visits, I sometimes feel there must be about 20 Jacqueline Wilson clones dashing up and down the country.' But luckily, however much in demand she is, nothing seems to stem the flow of creativity – and, of course, she's always got a pencil and paper handy.

Joanna Carey

Jacqueline Wilson began her writing career on the teenage magazine, Jackie. She had her first novel published at the age of 24, and has now written over 60 books. She has won many awards including the Children's Book Award (twice) and the Smarties Prize, and three of her books have been shortlisted for the Carnegie Medal, the most prestigious prize in children's publishing.

An interview with

Jacqueline Wilson

by Joanna Carey

With her long black skirt, short sharp hair and darkly varnished nails, Jacqueline Wilson (known to her friends as Jacky) has a precise, stylish individuality. She wears an array of rather gothic-looking silver rings (she buys one to celebrate publication of each of her novels – an idea she picked up from reading about E. Nesbit, one of her own favourite children's authors). Separated from her husband, she has one grown-up daughter and she lives alone in Kingston upon Thames in a small house with a vast and unruly collection of books.

*   *   *

My early childhood

When did you decide that you wanted to be a writer?

I always wanted to be a writer – even when I was little. I was an only child – even before I could write I would make up weird imaginary games, and as soon as I got involved in the world of books as a reader, I realized that I too wanted to be a writer.

Did your parents encourage you?

No! They just said 'Don't be silly – you'd have no chance coming from our sort of background!'

So what sort of background was it?

Jacqueline, aged one, with her mother and father.

My parents met in Bath, during the war. My father was a draughtsman and my mother was a clerical officer in the Admiralty. They met at a dance at the Pump

Room in Bath. They married, and I was conceived (by accident) shortly after. To begin with, they lived in furnished rooms in Bath, threatened with eviction if the baby cried. But luckily I was an obligingly silent baby.

Jacqueline with her Grandma and Grandpa.

Then we moved to Kingston upon Thames. My father was now working for the civil service, and we shared a house with my grandparents – my mum and dad and me upstairs, and my grandparents downstairs.

After this we rented rooms in Lewisham, and that's where I first started school. I had a tricky start at school, a lot of illness – measles, bronchitis, whooping cough. One of my first memories is crying at school dinners . . . we were given stew, mince and meat pies, which to me seemed strangely *exotic*. Like me, I'm afraid, my mother wasn't much of a cook and I was completely baffled by these meals. Then, at six, I moved to another school, Latchmere, where I settled in a bit better.

Were there any teachers you particularly remember?

Yes! Mr Townsend – he was gentle, kind, funny and artistic. He encouraged us to write and illustrate our own stories, and showed us his own paintings. And I remember – without any hint of anything unsuitable – being able to snuggle up to him. Another teacher was

Jacqueline (right) with her favourite teacher, Mr Townsend and another friend called Ann.

Mr Branson who, in some ways, was an excellent teacher (he got very good results at 11+) but he wasn't always fair.

I was a funny little kid, I was very curious about other people's lives, very observant of what was going on, and I thought very deeply about things but was usually too timid to *say* what I thought. One incident that particularly sticks in my mind concerned a girl called Christine with whom I had a passionate friendship. Christine's mother was dying of cancer and Christine, a middle child of three, was doing all the caring, and had a lot of responsibilities. She was exhausted. On this occasion we'd been having a 'heart-to-heart' in the loos and we were late for the lesson. I explained to Mr Branson that I'd been comforting Christine but he told us off, and I surprised myself by shouting at him. I told him he should have more consideration for Christine, what with her mother being so ill. He was unkind to other children too – he failed to nurture talent and humiliated one boy, Julian, by calling him 'clever clogs' and 'four-eyes'. But in some ways he was inspiring, especially when he read aloud to us on Fridays.

What about your other friends?

I was friendly with a lovely girl called Ann. I remember vividly the games we played in the playground in an imaginary treehouse. Ann had beautiful hair. I suppose I was obsessed with hair. I longed for plaits like my heroine, the child film star Mandy Miller, but my mother made me have my hair cut very short and

Jacqueline meeting her
childhood hero, the film
star Mandy Miller.

permed. (She would have liked a daughter like Shirley Temple.) I was teased mercilessly about my frizzy hair – and the way my school beret was jammed on top – 'Does your mum put your beret on with a battering ram?' someone once asked me.

I have strong memories of another girl, Pat, who was very large. I suppose it was a glandular problem, but anyway she was very fat and couldn't wear pretty clothes and was teased dreadfully. I was fascinated by her hair which was very long and always neatly plaited. Sometimes she'd let me undo her plaits and comb it out. We'd have quick snatched conversations in the corner of the cloakrooms, and I'd tell her how I liked her hair. I never joined in teasing her, but I still feel bad

Jacqueline in her
Latchmere school
uniform.

about the fact that I never actually stuck up for her. And then, one autumn term when we went back to school, the head told us that she had died during the summer holiday. I don't know what was wrong with her, but I remember she was sometimes a bit wheezy.

Another of the girls I remember from this time was Eileen, who had matured very early and actually had breasts and periods. Although she was the same age as me, she was like an incredibly glamorous big sister, instead of an ordinary friend.

And what about the boys in your class? Were you friendly with any of them?

Yes, there was a little gang of them I got on well with in top primary. There was Alan, David, Robert and Julian, the brainy one.

Jacqueline with her 'boyfriend' Alan.

What else do you remember about this school?

For some reason I remember being made Christmas card monitor for all the cards we sent each other within the school. I was trusted to take the cards to a special room where all sorts of things were stored. There was that smell of old milk-bottle tops, and costumes from long ago school plays. I invited some of the others in – my special friends – to dress up, and I put on a long purple velvet dress like a crinoline. It was a wonderful secret occasion.

What about home life? You were an only child - were you lonely? Were you allowed to have any pets?

By this time we were living in a council flat in Kingston where, apart from birds and fish, animals were not permitted. I longed for a dog, but the closest I got to that was a toy Pekinese that my mother bought me when I was eight. I called it Vip and I still have it.

Jacky leaves the room at this point and comes back with Vip – an elderly, but strangely life-like toy that has obviously been well looked after.

Vip was very real to me. He was my companion after school. I was the classic 'latch-key kid' with both parents at work. My dad was a civil servant, and my mum had a variety of jobs – working in a cake shop,

Jacqueline (second from left) and friends outside the flat in Kingston.

as a book keeper, and later on she became an antique dealer. Anyway, I always had to let myself in and get my own tea. Children had considerably more freedom in those days, but there were strict rules. Mum always warned me about 'strange men', and I wasn't allowed to do anything dangerous like switching on the cooker or the electric fire, or opening the door to anyone. I loved being by myself and didn't often feel lonely. I played endless, very complex imaginary games, and I read for hours and hours at a time.

So was it a happy childhood?

Sometimes it was, sometimes it wasn't! My parents simply didn't get on. They had nothing in common and there were lots of rows. I was an odd, nervy child. I had terrible nightmares and I have vivid memories of trying to stay awake to prevent them coming. I'd lie there for ages contemplating calling out for something to drink. My father would come in with a glass of water, and often things would be fine; but sometimes, for no apparent reason, he'd start shouting at me. I never knew what to expect. But he did read aloud to me. I can still remember the tone of his voice when he read me the childhood parts of *David Copperfield* and *The Faraway Tree* when I was very little. But he was a strange, worrying man. He was very moody and could go for weeks without talking. Sometimes he'd just look straight through me. I really didn't feel safe with him a lot of the time. But occasionally he did wonderful things. He'd take me on long country hikes and indulge my passion for imaginary games – something my mother would never do. She found 'imaginary' games tiresome and embarrassing. And sometimes he'd arrive home with marvellous books like *Marianne Dreams* by Catherine Storr, or *The*

Jacqueline playing with an imaginary friend at the seaside.

River by Rumer Godden. I've no idea where he got them, or who recommended them to him.

He wasn't a very good father, but later on, when I became a mother, he turned out to be a lovely gentle granddad. He never lost his temper with my daughter, Emma. He died when she was nine or ten and I'm really glad that before he died he had a 'second go', another chance to get it right.

Which other books do you remember from your childhood?

When I was very little I loved *Pookie, The Little White Rabbit* by Ivy M. Wallace, *The Shelf Animal* books, *The Flower Fairies*. When I could read properly, I raced through all of Noel Streatfeild's books, and I loved *The Family from One End Street*. Nobody's ever heard of my two favourite books, *Nancy and Plum* by Betty Macdonald and *Adventures with Rosalind* by Charlotte Austen. And then I read lots and lots of classics – *Little Women*, *What Katy Did*, *Black Beauty*. You automatically read all those classics in those days – you could get cheap editions at Woolworths. And my mother was very good – when I had finished reading just about everything in the children's library, she got permission for me to have early membership of the adult library. She was always very enterprising. Because I was mad about the actress Mandy Miller, she'd take me up to London, to Wardour Street in Soho, where the big film companies were, so I could get stills from my favourite movies. Although she didn't share my passion for books, she understood it – on holiday, my greatest treat was to be taken to secondhand book shops . . . and that's where I started this collection.

She gestures at the great wall of books, ancient and modern that dominates her living room.

* * *

My secondary school

What was your secondary school like?

Well, I failed my 11+ first time round, but passed it at a second attempt and was put in the 'grammar stream' of Coombe School, a new girls' comprehensive in New Malden. I hated Maths and PE, and my favourite subjects were Art and English. The English teacher was excellent, and introduced me to all sorts of exciting authors. But she was a stickler for things like spelling, grammar and structure. I remember getting my essays back with certain areas ringed in red pen and comments like 'slang!' and 'sloppy phrasing!' She'd probably have quite a few remarks to make about my work now!

The nicest teacher was the Art teacher. He was Polish. I particularly remember a day when I was made to stand outside the head's office as a punishment for not wearing my school beret. The Art teacher walked by and, seeing me standing there in disgrace, he winked at me and gave me a butterscotch.

And what about friends? How important were they?

My best friend then, at 11, was Chris – another Christine. It's the hair bit again I'm afraid. I was drawn to her by her long plaits. She'd let me brush them out and comb them. I'm still in touch with her. And then there was Carol. I liked her but she was rather moody, and she quickly overtook me in sophistication. I think the first year in secondary school is difficult, when children are reaching adolescence at different times – it's an uncomfortable stage as regards friends. But yes, I

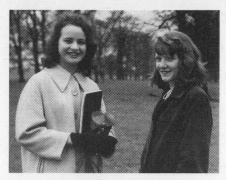

Jacqueline (left) with her
best friend Chris.

had friends. We used to hang around town in Kingston, or in the summer we'd go to the Surbiton Lagoon, a wonderful outdoor swimming pool (gone now, alas) where for something like sixpence – or maybe it was a shilling – you could stay all day. It was a great place for eyeing up the boys and there was a snack bar. It was heavenly.

And there was another girl called Cherry. I had to walk to school with her and we didn't get on too well, but I met up with her recently and found her to be a really interesting, gutsy personality. It's fascinating to meet up with old friends after a long time.

* * *

My career

When did you start writing?

I've always written. From the age of seven or eight I'd spend all my money on notebooks, and I wrote interminable stories throughout my childhood. I always kept diaries and I'd copy illustrations from books, and then write stories to go with them. I found Eve Garnett's drawings (*The Family from One End Street*) particularly inspiring – those children with droopy hems and plimsolls. I was really never without some kind of serial or story unfolding in my head. For further inspiration I used to get hold of old pattern books – *Style*, *Vogue* and *Simplicity* – which you could buy cheaply when the new ones came into our local department store, Bentalls. I'd cut out the fashion drawings of women and children and use them as characters in my stories. A slight drawback was that the only patterns for men were in the 'nightwear' section of the book, so all the men and boys I wrote about had to be wearing pyjamas and dressing gowns.

What did you do when you left school?

I left school at 16, because I didn't really like the school atmosphere. I'd like to have done A levels, but curiously, I had no idea that I could have gone on to a College of Further Education. My parents suggested I did a course in shorthand and typing, and I did that for a year before answering an advertisement asking for teenage writers. They accepted one of my stories and I was offered a job up in Dundee with DC Thompson, the publishers of many magazines and comics, including *Beano* and *Dandy*. I worked on a teenage magazine

Jacqueline (back row right) and the girls
who lived in the Church of Scotland Girls' Hostel.

called *Jackie* and women's magazines *Red Letter* and *Annabel*. It was brilliant training. I had to write all sorts of things – short stories, letters for the letters page and even the horoscope. I stayed in a Church of Scotland hostel, then together with another girl, moved out into

Jacqueline, aged 19, marrying Millar, aged 21.

digs. Then, at a dance, I met Millar – he was a printer – and quite soon we got engaged. We got married in 1965 and when Millar, who'd left school at 15, decided to join the police force we came down south, and moved in with my grandparents back in Kingston.

I was writing all the time now and had a part-time job in a bookshop. I got my first children's book, *Ricky's Birthday*, published by Macmillan in the Leila Berg series, Nippers, but they turned down my next one. I then wrote an adult novel about two girls who get kidnapped, and by chance it was put on the crime list.

So, making use of my police connection, I wrote a further four crime novels. But I knew that I really wanted to write for children. Indeed, all my crime novels had children as the main characters. This was the period when American 'teenage' novels, written in the first person, were coming to the fore, and in the late '70s I wrote *Nobody's Perfect*. I sent it to Macmillan but they rejected it, and there followed a sad and lonely time as I sent it off to one publisher after another, only to have it rejected. Then at last OUP accepted it and I got going.

In the '70s and '80s it was possible to write in far greater depth for teenagers than it is now. The books I wrote then were quite demanding, and dealt with all kinds of troubling subjects – sex, suicide, witchcraft – all kinds of things which, without wanting to sound precious, I wouldn't dream of touching now. I realize now that what's appropriate for a teenage market is also going to be read by children as young as nine.

I was then approached by Transworld to write for a younger age group (whilst keeping my teenage books with OUP) and that's when I started on the kind of books I'm currently writing. I was very glad that they agreed that the books should have illustrations – I've always agreed with Alice in Wonderland – 'What's the use of a book without pictures or conversation?' Having grown up with the illustrations of Eve Garnett (*The Family from One End Street*) and Ruth Gervis (*Ballet Shoes*), I particularly wanted black and white line drawings and I was delighted with the artistic marriage that Transworld arranged for me with the illustrator Nick Sharratt whose work was absolutely perfect from the start.

What makes Nick Sharratt such a good person to work with?

He is such a careful, sensitive reader of the text. He brings out all the details and adds his own

Jacqueline with her friend, Nick Sharrat.

magic touch. He doesn't ever resent my bossy suggestions, and comes up with his own ideas for the fantastic eye-catching cover illustrations. I feel so very lucky that Nick is still willing to do a double-act with me when he is so busy with his own great picture books.

When you are writing a book, is there a particular pattern to your day?

Yes. I swim first thing every day – fifty lengths of the local pool. Then I have breakfast, read the papers and attend to the post – just the business letters, that is. I get a huge number of letters from children, so I deal with those in the evening. At one point I thought I would have to get someone in to help me with the letters, or get a printed reply to send to each child, but really the letters are so touching, so extraordinary, so unpredictable and so funny (there was one the other day that started 'Dear Jacqueline Wilson, you are a goddess . . .'!), that I really do think that each child deserves a proper reply.

I get tremendous pleasure from all the letters I receive and from the knowledge that there are so many children wanting to be friends. It's a great privilege.

Where do you do your writing?

It varies – sometimes upstairs at my desk, sometimes at the kitchen table, sometimes curled up in an armchair. But really I can write anywhere, which is lucky because I have to write every single day. For me, one of the very worst things about being a writer is the fear that suddenly one day I'll find that I'm no longer able to do

Jacqueline at her desk.

it. I get so worried I might somehow lose it, that even when I'm on holiday I do at least 15 minutes every day. I don't have any problem about *where* I do it, which is fortunate because I've been travelling so much recently that most of my writing has been on train journeys! Even on a short trip like Surbiton to Waterloo, I can write 500 words without being distracted by what's going on round me. I write in longhand – I've got really squiggly little writing and then type it up myself at home on an old Olivetti manual typewriter. Yes, everybody is surprised that I don't use a computer. I'm sure that one day I shall but I keep putting off the moment.

And do you do much rewriting?

I never rewrite as I go along or I'd never progress at all! With every book there comes a point, about halfway through, when I suddenly think – oh help, this is rubbish! Nobody's going to want to read this! But I've learnt to take no notice of those thoughts and I just carry on. I always leave it for a bit when I've finished, and then do the rewriting.

Why do you write for children?

Jacqueline playing with
her dolls on her
grandmother's doorstep.

Because, in almost every way, children interest me more than adults. I've always collected children's books – and I've always collected dolls, too.

A peep over the great wall of books reveals a whole army of dolls lined up on a sofa – antique Victorian dolls, dolls of all nations, Barbie dolls, the lot.

I find it easiest to write from a child's point of view. I just start off in the first person and 'become' the child I'm writing about.

And nowadays, of course, I also spend a huge amount of time with children, visiting schools, and that way I learn at first hand about their current preoccupations, fashions, language, etc. I have to be careful with current slang as it changes so quickly and easily looks dated.

Your books consistently address difficult themes – homelessness, bullying, sibling rivalry, delinquency, divorce and step families, mental illness.
Are you always on the lookout for such themes?

No! I certainly don't think of them as 'issue-led' books. That approach would result in the books being turgid, didactic and just plain boring. Yes, I agree, the children in my books do have problems, but I don't go hunting for them, the problems emerge as the characters take shape, as the story itself develops. And although difficult situations arise in the stories, I'm always amazed at how bright children are, and how quickly they get what I'm on about.

To what extent has your daughter affected your writing career?

Emma was a very imaginative little girl. I made up endless stories for her – stories full of detail with lots of birthdays, lots of descriptions and happy endings. That's what she liked. When we had to do something boring

Jacqueline and daughter, Emma.

like food shopping, we'd play imaginary games, pretending to be other people – Emma would be a grown-up lady called Angela, and I was her little girl, Rosie. She was fascinated by the Victorian period, and loved stories about it. She had an Edwardian shop, and I made little cardboard figures who went shopping there. We're still best friends now she's grown up – we chat on the phone for hours and send each other a postcard every day. She's a lecturer in French at Cambridge, a Fellow of Corpus Christi, an author of academic books and she's a daughter in a million. She's been heroic enough to find the time to read everything I've written, and is hugely supportive.

How do you relax? Is music important to you?

I play a lot of records. I like medieval chants while I'm writing – if it's in Latin the words don't distract. Otherwise I play Queen – I was a great fan of Freddie Mercury. I like country music – Hank Wangford, Mary Chapin Carpenter, Willie Nelson and I love Dory Previn and Dusty Springfield.

And what about painting?

The walls of Jacqueline's house are covered with paintings, postcard reproductions, exhibition posters and cuttings.

I'm very interested in painting. I learnt a lot about art history while my daughter was growing up – we made regular visits to the galleries and still do [*she turns round to show me the other side of her 'Look Back in Ingres' T-shirt from the National Gallery*] and we went to lots of lectures.

Cinema and television?

I love the cinema. I suppose my favourite film now would be *Thelma and Louise* – as a child it was *Mandy*. I don't watch a lot of television, but I like certain documentaries and things like *ER* and *Friends*.

And what about sport?

I don't play any games. I was rather a disappointment to my father – he was quite sporty, and I think I let him down when he took me to the tennis club he'd joined.

Swimming's the only sport I enjoy, unless you count line dancing which I love – you don't need a partner and you can be any age. But my greatest relaxation is reading.

What sort of a future do you see for books in the face of modern technology? Will children still be reading in 50 years' time?

I think that the phenomenal success of J. K. Rowling and her Harry Potter books has proved that if the books

Jacqueline in her living room, surrounded by books.

are good, children will read them! I suppose there will
be changes eventually in how people access literature,
but there's always going to be a hunger for stories in
one form or another.

Which book - either children's or adult - has had the greatest influence on you?

Rather surprisingly perhaps, it's *Lolita*. My father
bought it, thinking it would be a good sexy read I
suppose, and I found it. I was 13, and I read it secretly,
with a Catherine Cookson dust jacket round it. What

Jacqueline with her friends, Rebecca and Hannah.

astonished me was the language. I was amazed by the power – the possibilities of language, the magic of prose. That interested me deeply. At the time it really opened my eyes.

And of all your own books, which is your favourite?

I think *Double Act* because it's about twins. I've always been intrigued by twins, and to write about these identical children who were in fact totally different was such a challenge. I really enjoyed writing it. And

The Illustrated Mum was a challenge too. I was anxious about that. Because it was such a dark subject I did wonder about the reaction, but it's been tremendously rewarding to get letters from children who understand what it's all about.

What's the best thing about being a writer?

What I love is the fact that I have two lives. When things go wrong in real life it's good to know that I can lose myself in an imaginary world. I love that. It's a wonderful escape.

Your books have become a colossal success. Has that been a surprise?

Yes! Obviously I hoped for success, but I never really believed it would happen. It's extraordinary. I went on a school visit the other day, and as I entered the playground children started squealing and running towards me screaming. I felt like a sort of Granny

Spice! A lot of my success is due to the children themselves. Children are a hugely effective sales force; and since I joined Transworld, and my books have become more widely available – in WH Smith, for example – things have really taken off. But no, I never anticipated this kind of success. It's as if there's another person called Jacqueline Wilson and it doesn't seem to be me!

What are your top ten favourite books and why?

Nancy and Plum by Betty Macdonald
I read this story about two orphan sisters at least 20 times throughout my childhood.

Ballet Shoes by Noel Streatfeild
This book made me desperate to learn ballet myself. I used to pretend my pink bedroom slippers were ballet shoes.

The Family from One End Street by Eve Garnett

I loved this story – and carefully coloured in all the detailed illustrations.

What Katy Did by Susan Coolidge
The children in this book are so real. I felt particularly sorry for odd little Elsie.

Little Women by Louisa M. Alcott
One of my favourite books. It was a treat visiting Louisa M. Alcott's house in Concord when I was on holiday in New England.

The Bell Jar by Sylvia Plath
My favourite modern novel, sharp and savage and sad.

The collected stories of Katherine Mansfield
I love them all, especially the ones about children.

Lolita by Vladimir Nabokov
Brilliantly written, though disturbing.

To the Lighthouse by Virginia Woolf

She's not an easy read but she's so worth the struggle.

Jane Eyre by Charlotte Brontë

Jane is a wonderfully original character. I think this is the oddest but most absorbing love story of all time.

Jacqueline's Books

An overview by Joanna Carey

One of the secrets of Jacqueline Wilson's success
is her easy ability to express things entirely from
a child's point of view – and to give a real voice
to the 8–12 year olds she writes about, whatever
their circumstances. Divorce, dysfunctional
families, poverty, homelessness, redundancy,
bullying, social inequality, bereavement,
juvenile delinquency, mental illness and
anorexia are just some of the issues that crop up
in her hugely readable, funny, thought-
provoking novels. These are books that reflect
the times we live in, and children relate
instantly to the immediacy – and the content –

of Jacqueline's books.

Exploring our imperfect world

Bad Girls, published in 1996, is about a friendship between two very different girls. Mandy, the ten-year-old narrator, is very young for her age and has an embarrassingly over-protective mother. Babied at home and bullied at school, she's thrilled to make friends with Tanya who, although alarmingly streetwise and light-fingered, is warm-hearted. The story is about the very touching relationship that develops. I reviewed it in *The Guardian* and almost immediately received an indignant letter from a man who had bought it, on my recommendation, for his granddaughter. He'd opened it at random on his way home from the shop and had chanced upon a passage where Tanya talks about her mother's suicide: 'she topped herself . . . Well, she was always a bit zonked out of her brains anyway . . . '

The man was horrified. 'You should have mentioned this in your review, ' he wrote. 'It's no subject for a nine year old to be reading about. Surely children should be shielded from that kind of thing.' Then two days later, he wrote again. Oh help, I thought, I suppose he's got to the bit where the girls get arrested for shoplifting. But in fact he was writing to say he'd been a bit hasty in his criticism of the book. He, and the granddaughter, had now read it properly. He could see now, he said, how it was necessary to mention Tanya's mum's suicide – it was clear how the awful events in her life had caused her behaviour problems. Furthermore, his granddaughter had pointed out how the friendship between the girls was important to them both. 'It's not much like the books I read as a child,' he went on, 'but it certainly makes you think! We enjoyed it and my wife's reading it now.'

And his letter made me think too: with tabloid newspapers, television, videos and the internet all easy to access, there's almost nothing that children can be shielded from today. Shocking news reports, unsolved crimes and inexplicably bizarre characters daily flash before our eyes, so it's important for children to have access to entertaining fiction – like Jacqueline's – that allows them to explore our imperfect world, to discuss what's right and what's wrong, to put bewildering events into some kind of context and to see how chaotic situations can usually be worked out.

The importance of illustration

In the '80s Jacqueline wrote novels for older children like *Nobody's Perfect*, *Falling Apart*, and *The Dream Palace* which were published by OUP. These were quite long books, densely written and purposefully 'literary'. But when she moved to Transworld to write for a younger age group, she seemed to reinvent herself with a simple direct style that has won her a huge following. Remembering from her own childhood the importance of simple line drawings, like those by Eve Garnett in *The Family from One End Street*, or Ruth Gervis in *Ballet Shoes*, when she joined Transworld Jacqueline was keen that black and white illustrations should be an integral part of her books.

Her partnership with the artist Nick Sharratt gives her books a unifying identity and a visual framework for the structure of each story. His drawings extend the narrative in a number of ways, adding details, breaking up dense areas of text with comic sketches, clarifying complex passages with explanatory drawings, and visualizing fantasies – like Tracy Beaker's wild imaginings about her mother, for example – with an engagingly mischievous wit.

Jacqueline's storytellers

The age group these novels are aimed at is roughly 8–12, although of course there are huge variations in the speed at which children normally develop. Normality itself is a variable concept, and at the age of 10 say, in terms of personal development, family background and environment, normality is simply what you are familiar with. Each child is different, but as Jacqueline's characters demonstrate, around this age, when they still enjoy imaginative play, and before they have to cope with puberty and the pressure to conform, children are astonishingly resourceful and frighteningly observant.

All the books are written from the point of view of the child, and in each story the chirpy individuality of the opening paragraphs immediately brings you close to the narrator. *The Story of Tracy Beaker* starts off with Tracy (astonishingly resourceful, frighteningly observant) having to fill in a questionnaire about herself at the children's home where she lives.

ABOUT ME:

I am 10 years 2 months old. My birthday is on 8 May. It's not fair because that dopey Peter Ingham has his birthday then too, so we just got the one cake between us. And we had to hold the knife to cut the cake together. Which meant we only had half a wish each. Wishing is for babies anyway. They don't come true.

THE PEOPLE IN MY FAMILY ARE:

My mum. I don't have a dad. I lived with my mum when I was little and we got on great but then she got this Monster Gorilla Boyfriend and I hated him and he hated me back and he beat me up and so I had to be taken into care. No wonder my mum sent him packing.

MY OWN FAMILY LIVE AT:

I'm not sure exactly where my mum lives now because she has to keep moving about because she gets fed up living in one place too long.

MY FOSTER FAMILY:

There's no point filling this bit in. I haven't got a foster family at the moment.

I've had two . . . Aunty Peggy and Uncle Sid first . . . then Julie and Ted. They were young and friendly and they bought me a bike . . . I thought I'd be staying with them until my mum came to get me for good but then. . . I don't want to write about it. It ended up with me getting turfed out THROUGH NO FAULT OF MY OWN. I was so mad I smashed up the bike so I don't even have that any more.

Few writers could match the stunning economy of this story-telling. The gaping holes that Tracy leaves in her account of her life and the terrifyingly vivid details she does include make reading this book a very creative, imaginative and often wildly funny experience. Highly imaginative and shamelessly manipulative, Tracy leaves no stone unturned in her search for a good foster family. It's a truly heart-rending tale, and with the reckless intensity of Tracy's non-stop narrative, it's hilarious, sad and shocking by turns, but hugely optimistic and never, never sentimental.

Authors who use child narrators always run the risk of either slowing up the story by letting the child ramble on realistically, or making that child implausibly articulate. With crafty artistic licence and convincing speech rhythms, Jacqueline combines these techniques to make her characters entirely believable. She never allows the fact that it's a child speaking to prevent the expression of complex thoughts and ideas. Her characters sometimes use rather sophisticated words, like 'corpulent', 'squandering' and 'absolutely devastated', and there's a hint of the immortal *Just William* when Tracy Beaker talks about the dangers of being 'institutionalized . . . I know what it means and all. I've heard Elaine and some of the social workers going on about it. It's when you get so used to living in an institution like this that you never learn how to live in a proper home.'

Jacqueline always includes lots of jokes, figures of speech and entertaining word play, and in places she hands over to her illustrator who, with a little drawing, will show what's meant when someone has a 'sharp tongue' or 'puts their foot down'.

She's good too on the day-to-day paraphernalia of a child's life – the little toys and hair decorations, scrunchies and slides, the dolls, the sets of felt tips, the drawing books and the glorious variety of junk food and sherbert saucers, fizzy cola bottles and long red jelly snakes.

Many of the children Jacqueline writes about are those who, through no fault of their own, are socially marooned, set apart from the rest, identified (and often stigmatised) by their particular circumstances – like Tracy, who has to live in a children's home, or Elsa in *The Bed and Breakfast Star*, whose family has become homeless, or Andy in *The Suitcase Kid*.

The Suitcase Kid is so named because poor Andy has to spend so much time packing up her things to travel between two homes. Her parents have split up and have new relationships, so Andy ends up with two new step parents, five new siblings and two new homes, when all she really wants is to be with her own mum and dad, in their old home, Mulberry Cottage. It's a desperately poignant story about a situation that will be familiar to thousands of children. And though there's a real feeling of the misery and the bitter arguments between the parents, Jacky ingeniously divides the story up into short scenes which acknowledge but never dwell on the more uncomfortable events. This story is a masterpiece in every way and Andy's loneliness, her grief and incomprehension at the loss of her former life are unforgettable. There's a strong fairytale element throughout Jacqueline's books, and the magical fantasies Andy weaves around her little toy rabbit are treated with great sensitivity and compassion.

While most of these books have one central character, whom the reader can react to and identify with, *Double Act* is a bit different. Ruby and Garnet are identical twins. Their mum has died and they are reluctant to accept their dad's new partner. *Double Act* is much more demanding of its readers as, instead of simply addressing the reader, the twins also bounce their opinions off each other as their personalities develop and diverge, and their lives begin to follow different paths. The text uses two different typefaces – bold for Ruby, the dominant twin, and delicate italics for Garnet who is more thoughtful and quieter than her sister . . . ('"That's because I can't get a word in edgeways," says Garnet.') Even the illustrations are shared out between two artists.

One effect of a story that's told entirely from the point of view of just one character is the relentless intensity that builds up. Think of Tracy Beaker yacking away nineteen to the dozen even when she's in bed, or Elsa in *The Bed and Breakfast Star* who simply can't stop telling jokes, and there's sometimes a need for a gear change, an opportunity to slow up. Throughout these stories there are some valuable oases of calm when the girls do drawings, make up stories, sing, make cakes or even play 'television', acting out scenes from *Friends* or *Neighbours*.

In *The Lottie Project* the narrator is Charlie, a

bright, observant, articulate eleven year old who has a strong, positive relationship with her single mum, Jo.

> *Jo and I haven't always had a home. We lived with Grandma and Grandpa at first. That was pretty bad. Grandma is the sort of lady who keeps a damp flannel neatly folded in a plastic bag and she's forever whipping it out and smearing round imaginary sticky bits. On me. Even at my age. That's nothing. She does it to Jo too.*

The story steps neatly back through the generations to reveal an unexpected dimension. When Charlie (reluctantly at first) gets involved with a school history project, a fascinating, thought-provoking parallel story emerges set in Victorian times.

Boys and beauty

Aside from her books for younger readers, like *Cliffhanger* and *Buried Alive*, boys are comparatively few and far between in Jacqueline's books until *Girls Under Pressure* and *Girls in Love*. Even then, though they may set a few hearts racing, the boys get little more than walk-on parts. Just as she allows her ten-year-olds to make the most of their childhood, Jacqueline is careful not to hurry the older girls into romantic situations. She takes quite a hard line on the way girls are too often expected to conform to the physical stereotypes in fashion magazines. Mr Windsor, the splendid Art teacher in *Girls in Love* is keen to show the girls some alternative images of woman. He shows them paintings by Frida Kahlo and Paula Rego and valiantly makes the case for big women when he talks about the old masters.

"You girls! You're all brainwashed! . . .

Titian liked large firm women with big bottoms. Rubens liked his women large too, but wobbly. Goya's women were white and slender, then Renoir liked them very big and salmon pink."

Covered all over with tattoos, Marigold, in *The Illustrated Mum*, doesn't conform to any conventional ideas of beauty – or motherhood. This is a dark, uncompromising novel: Marigold is a tragic, eccentric character, suffering from a severe mental illness with violent mood swings and heavy drinking. Dolphin, aged ten, and her older sister Star have to treat their mum like a wayward child as they struggle to survive. Naturally their school life is disrupted:

Next morning . . . Marigold was locked in the bathroom being sick so we couldn't have a proper wash and I had to walk to school clenching hard, a pain in my

tummy I needed to pee so badly. I was
terrified I wouldn't make it, especially the
last few seconds as I dashed to the girls'
toilets and got the cubicle open and my
knickers down – but I was just about OK.

The other girls tease Dolphin – and not just
about her name:

"Bottle Nose lives in a squat," says
Kayleigh, [as Dolphin has a wash in
the school sink] . . . *"I bet they haven't*
even GOT a sink at home."

"I do NOT live in a squat, Monkey
Bum," I said fiercely, although we'd lived
in several squats in the past. One of them
didn't have a sink. Someone had smashed
it up, and the toilet too, so we had to use an
Elsan. That was the squat where Marigold
had the worst boyfriend of all . . .

But Dolphin is used to this, and at ten she accepts and loves her mother unconditionally. Star, however, who is older, is increasingly ashamed and intolerant of Marigold's shambolic behaviour, and her obsession with tattoos:

"You said it was sick and pathetic getting yourself tattooed again and again. You said you'd save up for laser treatment to get them removed . . . they make you look like a circus freak . . . why can't you act NORMAL?"

"I don't want to be normal," said Marigold. "I can't figure out why you do all of a sudden. What's the matter with you, Star?"

Dolphin is the narrator of this sad, engrossing story, and in contrast to the frantic pace of *Tracy Beaker* or *Double Act*, hers is a calmer delivery that allows the story a lot more breadth, which it certainly needs. It's a shocking, many-layered novel, an emotional roller coaster that is compulsively readable at a number of different levels of understanding.

While Jacqueline's strikingly individual central characters all share roughly the same kind of background – usually in an urban setting, with varying degrees of social, economic and emotional insecurity – her readers are increasingly wide ranging. She's one of an important band of contemporary authors who really have made reading a serious option for children who previously would never have turned to books for entertainment.

Joanna Carey

2000

Bibliography

In date order

The Werepuppy

Blackie 1991 (hb), Puffin 1993 (pb), illustrated by

Janet Robertson

Micky knew he shouldn't have watched the video with his sisters. Now every dog he sees reminds him of the terrifying werewolves, and he's even frightened of his grandmother's old fur cape. Mum decides the only answer is to get Micky a puppy of his own. But she didn't know he would choose a werepuppy. Wolfie turns out to be a very special pet – and a real joker.

The Story of Tracy Beaker

Doubleday 1991 (hb), Yearling 1992 (pb), illustrated by Nick Sharratt

Tracy Beaker is ten years old. She lives in a children's home but desperately wants a real home with a real family. This is the story of how she sets about achieving that dream with her irrepressible humour and determination.

Shortlisted for the Smarties Prize 1991/Carnegie Medal 1991

Video Rose

Puffin 1992 (pb)

When the video breaks down, a strange old man comes to mend it. Suddenly Rose can rewind and fast-forward her own life!

The Suitcase Kid

Yearing 1993 (pb), illustrated by Nick Sharratt

When her parents divorce, Andy hates being part of

two new families.

Winner of the Children's Book Award 1993

Take a Good Look

Puffin 1993 (pb)

Mary may not be able to see properly, but she's determined to go out alone. Her adventure turns to nightmare as she gets caught up in a robbery.

Freddy's Teddy
Teddy at the Fair
Teddy Goes Swimming
Come Back Teddy!

Longman Book Project 1994

Four beginning-to-read stories about a small boy and his teddy.

Mum-minder

Yearling 1994 (pb), illustrated by Nick Sharratt

Can nine-year-old Sadie cope when her child-minder mum is taken ill over the half-term holiday?

Shortlisted for the Writers' Guild Award 1993

Werepuppy on Holiday

Blackie 1994 (hb), Puffin 1995 (pb), illustrated by Janet Robertson

Only Micky knows that his pet dog Wolfie is really a werepuppy – a baby werewolf, whose middle name is trouble! When Wolfie is banned from the family holiday, Micky can't believe it. What fun is a holiday without Wolfie?

Mark Spark in the Dark

Puffin 1994 (pb)

Mark Spark is bursting with bright ideas – he comes up with a brilliant idea to raise money for Guide Dogs for the Blind. But when it comes to conquering his fear of the dark, it is his almost blind Great Gran who can teach him a thing or two.

Jimmy Jelly

Piccadilly 1995 (hb), Barn Owl Books 1999 (pb), illustrated by Lucy Keijser

Rosie and Mum hate Jimmy Jelly's television programme. But they hate him all the more when he's there – with Angela – all the time. Then the real Jimmy Jelly comes to the shopping centre and everyone's in for a BIG surprise.

Cliffhanger

Yearling 1995 (pb), illustrated by Nick Sharratt

From climbing and abseiling to canoeing and a Crazy Bucket Race, the adventure holiday promises to be full of action. There's just one problem as far as Tim is concerned: he is hopeless at sports of any kind . . .

The Bed and Breakfast Star

Yearling 1995 (pb), illustrated by Nick Sharratt

Life in the Royal Hotel – a run-down bed and breakfast hotel for homeless families – is no joke for Elsa and her family. But when things go dangerously wrong, Elsa suddenly has the chance to be a real star.

Shortlisted for the Carnegie Medal 1995, the Young Telegraph/Fully Booked Award 1995 and the Nottinghamshire Children's Book Award.

The Dinosaur's Packed Lunch

Doubleday 1995 (hb), Corgi 1996 (pb), illustrated by Nick Sharratt

On a school trip to see the dinosaurs in the museum, everyone in the class has a packed lunch – except for Dinah. That is, until a friendly iguanadon decides to help. Soon Dinah has a very special packed lunch – and a huge surprise to come!

Double Act

Doubleday 1995 (hb), Yearling 1996 (pb), illustrated by
Nick Sharratt

Ruby and Garnet are identical twins. They do everything together, especially since their mother died three years earlier. But can being a double act work for ever? So much around them is changing – beginning with Dad and his new friend Rose.

Winner of the Smarties Prize 1995 and the Children's Book Award 1996; highly recommended for the Carnegie Medal; shortlisted for the Young Telegraph/Fully Booked Award 1996.

Twin Trouble

Mammoth 1996 (pb), illustrated by Philippe Dupasquier

Connie doesn't like it when the new twins come home. She wishes it would be just her, Mum and Dad. But when her magic beads click together, suddenly the baby twins don't seem so bad after all.

Glubbslyme

Yearling 1995 (pb), illustrated by Jane Cope

When Rebecca wades into the witch's pond after a row with her best friend Sarah, she meets a very unusual new friend – a huge warty toad called Glubbslyme. Hundreds of years old, he can talk and – best of all – he can work magic. Maybe he can help Rebecca be best friends with Sarah again.

My Brother Bernardette

Heinemann Young Books 1995 (hb), illustrated by
Stephen Lewis

Poor Bernard. It's the summer camp but he doesn't want to play football and join drama class like all the other kids. All he wants to do is design clothes. Everybody teases him until they realize just how much they need him.

Beauty and the Beast

Black 1996 (pb)

A witty play where the Beast turns out to be a giant slug with a slime problem.

Mr Cool

Kingfisher 1996 (pb), illustrated by Stephen Lewis

A jokey story about a rock band with one seriously uncool member called Kevin.

Bad Girls

Doubleday 1996 (hb), Yearling 1997 (pb), illustrated by
Nick Sharratt

Mum says Mandy's new friend Tanya is a bad influence, but Mandy is sure she isn't really bad . . .

Winner of the Sheffield Children's Book Award 1997 shorter novel category; shortlisted for the Carnegie Medal 1997

The Monster Story-teller

Doubleday 1997 (hb), Corgi 1997 (pb), illustrated by
Nick Sharratt

Natalie is fed up. The lesson is boring and Mr Hunter won't let her tell stories. But then she notices the monster living in the plant pot at the back of the class. It is waving at her . . .

The Lottie Project

Doubleday 1997 (hb), Yearling 1998 (pb), illustrated by
Nick Sharratt

Charlie thought history was really boring until she started her project on the Victorians and discovered Lottie, her double.

Connie and the Water Babies

Mammoth 1997 (pb), illustrated by Georgien Overwater

Connie isn't scared of the video recorder, a baby gerbil or the dentist, like the grown-ups in her family. But she does have one phobia – water. Can a special magic cure her once and for all?

Girls in Love

Doubleday 1997 (hb), Corgi 1998 (pb), illustrated by
Nick Sharratt

Meet Ellie, Magda and Nadine. Three friends. All different, but with one thing in common. They'd like a boyfriend . . .

Buried Alive!

Doubleday 1998 (hb), Yearling 1999 (pb), illustrated by Nick Sharratt and Sue Heap

Tim and Biscuits are on holiday and facing a Deadly Enemy. Two, in fact – the bullies Pinch-Face and Pickle-Head.

Winner of the Sheffield Children's Book Award 1999 shorter novel category

Girls Under Pressure

Doubleday 1998 (hb), Corgi 1999 (pb)

Ellie's obsession with her weight threatens to develop
into an eating disorder, but her friends Magda and
Nadine have problems of their own to cope with.

Rapunzel

Hippo 1998 (pb), illustrated by Nick Sharratt

The great traditional story of Rapunzel, the baby stolen
by a witch and imprisoned in a high tower, retold in
Jacqueline Wilson's inimitable style.

The Illustrated Mum

Doubleday 1999 (hb), Yearling 2000 (pb), illustrated by
Nick Sharratt

Covered in tattoos, Marigold is no one's idea of a normal
mother, but her daughter Dolphin loves her dearly.
Unfortunately Dolphin's older sister, Star, is becoming
increasingly annoyed by Marigold's irresponsible

behaviour, especially when she forgets to buy food and leaves them alone all night.

Winner of the NIBBY Children's Book of the Year; shortlisted for the Whitbread Children's Book of the Year Award and the Carnegie Medal

How to Survive Summer Camp

OUP 1999 (pb), illustrated by Sue Heap

Typical! Mum and Uncle Bill have gone off on a swanky honeymoon, while Stella's been dumped at Evergreen Summer Camp. Sharing a room with two unbearable snobs, it looks like she's in for a nightmare summer – how can Stella possibly survive?

Monster Eyeballs

Heinemann Young Books 1999 (hb), (pb), illustrated by Stephen Lewis

Kate likes school. The only bad thing is Mark, the class bully. He's always stealing Kate's things and playing tricks on her. But when he arrives at Kate's house for her brother's birthday party, she has a chance to turn the tables on him.

Girls Out Late

Doubleday 1999 (hb)

While out with her friends drop-dead gorgeous Magda and super-cool Nadine, plain plump Ellie meets Russell who actually seems interested in her. But will he stay interested in a girl who has to be home by nine?

The Dare Game

Doubleday 2000 (hb), Yearling 2001 (pb)

The sequel to *The Story of Tracy Beaker* sees Tracy firmly established in the home of foster mother Cam. But not everything is how Tracy imagined it would be, and she's particularly upset that Cam refuses to spend loads of money on her! Defiant Tracy bunks off school and forms a friendship with two very different boys based on playing *The Dare Game*, which gets more and more dangerous . . .

Lizzie Zipmouth

Young Corgi 2000 (pb)

Lizzie refuses to speak. It's as if she has a zip across her mouth. She doesn't want to talk to anyone, especially her new stepbrothers and their dad. She certainly doesn't feel like talking to her mum. Then one day a member of her new family turns out to be even more stubborn than Lizzie, and things begin to change . . .

Vicky Angel

Doubleday 2000 (hb), Yearling 2001 (pb)

Jade can hardly believe it when her best friend Vicky dies in a tragic accident. But Vicky is not going to let being dead stop her! Wherever Jade is and whatever she's doing, Vicky makes her presence felt.

The Cat Mummy

Doubleday 2001 (hb), Yearling 2002 (pb)

Verity's tabby cat, Mabel, is old and smells a bit, but is much loved all the same. More importantly, Mabel once belonged to Verity's mum, who died when Verity was born. Verity gets twitchy about visiting her grave, which makes her think about being in the ground with a head of full of worms. So when she finds Mabel dead in the wardrobe, it seems a much better idea to take a few lessons from the Ancient Egyptians and mummify Mabel so they can be together forever . . .

Dustbin Baby

Doubleday 2001 (hb)

April Showers (so called because of her birth date, April 1st, and her tendency to burst into tears at the drop of a hat) was discovered as a newborn baby in a dustbin. Her young life has passed by in a blur of ever-changing foster homes, but after a row on her 14th birthday, she decides it is time to find out the truth about her real family.

Sleep-Overs

Doubleday 2001 (hb), Galaxy 2002 (pb)

New-girl in school Daisy is finding her feet, slowly becoming 'one of the gang' who take it in turns to have sleep-over parties. But when it comes to her turn to play host, Daisy is forced to tell her new friends about her mentally and physically disabled older sister. Daisy worries that for snide bully Chloe, this is just the excuse she needs to elbow Daisy out.

Secrets

Doubleday 2002 (hb)

Treasure lives on the local council estate with her loving and capable grandmother. She is devoted to her nan but lives in fear of having to go back to live with her mother and violent stepfather. When Treasure has to run away to avoid her stepfather, her friend India comes up with a hiding place inspired by her favourite author, Anne Frank.

The Bad Sister

Jacqueline Wilson

It's a beautiful gravestone. A little girl angel spreads her wings, head shyly lowered, neat stone curls never in need of brushing. Her robe is ornately tucked and gathered, a little fancy for an angel frock, as if she's about to attend a heavenly party.

I step over the miniature rosebush and feel along the carving on the gravestone with one finger. I whisper the name.

Angela Robinson.

My name.

Beloved Daughter.

Not me.

Born 1976. Died 1983.

My sister. She died in 1983. I was born in 1984, eleven months later. Another Angela, to replace the first. I suppose that was the theory. Only it hasn't worked out that way. I'm not a little angel.

I reach out and snap the gravestone angel hard on her perky little nose. She smiles serenely back at me, above retaliation. I hit her harder, wanting to push her right off her pedestal. A woman tending a nearby grave looks up, startled. I blush and pretend to be buffing up the angel's cheeks with the palm of my hand.

I haven't been here for a while. Mum used to take me week in, week out, every single Sunday when I was little. I took my Barbie dolls and some scraps of black velvet and played funerals. My prettiest bride Barbie got to be Angela. I sometimes pinned paper-hankie wings on her and made her flap through the air in holy splendour.

One time I dressed her in a nightie and wrapped her up in a plastic carrier bag and started to dig a little hole, all set to bury her. Mum turned round from tidying Angela's flowers and was appalled.

'You can't dig here. This is a cemetery!' she said.

The cemetery seemed a place purpose-built for digging, though I knew enough not to point this out. Mum was going through a bad patch. Sometimes she seemed normal, like anyone else's mum, *my* mum. Then she'd suddenly burst into tears and start a crying spell.

I was always frightened by her tears. There was nothing decorous about her grief. Her eyes were bleary and bloodshot, her face damp and greasy, her mouth almost comically square. I'd try putting my arms round her. She didn't ever push me away but she didn't always gather me up and rock me. Sometimes she scarcely seemed to notice I was there.

She still has crying spells now, even though Angela has been dead for fifteen years. I'll invite Vicky or Sarah home from school and we'll discover Mum crying in the kitchen, head half-hidden in the dishtowel. Birthdays are bad times too. And Christmas is the worst. Angela died in December. A quick dash, an icy road, a car that couldn't brake in time.

One Christmas Mum got so crazy she bought two sets of presents. One pile of parcels for me, one for my dead sister. I don't know how Mum thought she was going to give the first Angela her presents. She could hardly lob them right up to Heaven. I imagined Angela up on her cloud, playing with her big blue teddy and her Little Mermaid doll and her giant rainbow set of felt-tip pens.

After a few weeks my own teddy's plush was matted, I'd given my Little Mermaid doll an unflattering haircut, and I'd pressed too hard on my favourite purple pen so that it wouldn't colour neatly any more. The first Angela's presents stayed pristine.

The first Angela didn't leave the bath tap running so that there was a flood and the kitchen ceiling fell down. The first Angela didn't get into fights at school and poke out her tongue at the teacher. The first Angela didn't bite her nails and tell fibs and wet the bed.

My grandma actually told me to ask Angela for help, as if she'd already acquired saintly status.

'Pray to your sister to help you stop having temper

tantrums. Ask Angela for advice on how to stop biting your nails. See if Angela can help you with wetting the bed, your poor mother can't cope with all the extra laundry.'

Dad got furious when he found out, and he and Grandma had a big row. Then Mum and Dad argued too, and for a little while Dad wouldn't let me see Grandma any more. We didn't often see my other gran or any of Dad's family – I think someone had said something tactless about my name way back at my christening and Mum wouldn't speak to them again.

We're still not on really friendly terms with the family – so it was a surprise when the wedding invitation came through the letterbox this morning. Mum opened it and stared, fingering the deckle-edge.

'What is it?' I asked.

'Nothing,' said Mum. She tied to crumple it up, but it was too stiff.

Dad looked up from his newspaper.

'Is that a wedding invitation?' he said. 'Let's have a look.'

'It's nothing,' Mum repeated, but Dad reached across and snatched it from her.

'Good lord! Becky's getting married,' said Dad.

'My cousin Becky?' I said. 'The one that used to be best friends with Angela?'

Dad usually frowns at me when I mention the first Angela because he doesn't want to set Mum off – but now he just nodded.

'And we're invited to the wedding?' I said. I got up and peered over Dad's shoulder. 'To the ceremony. And the wedding breakfast. Doesn't that sound weird? It's not a real breakfast, is it, like bacon and egg? And a disco in the evening. So . . . are we going?'

'I don't think so,' said Mum.

'I think we ought to go,' said Dad.

'You go if you want. But I don't think I can face it,' said Mum, rubbing her eyebrows with her thumb and forefinger, the way she always does when she has a headache. 'Angela and Becky were just like sisters.'

'So why shouldn't we see Becky married? I've hated the way we've barely seen the family all these years. I know it's painful, I know it brings back memories – but life goes *on*. It's not fair to me to cut me off from my family. And it's not fair to Angela either.'

'Not fair to *Angela?*' said Mum. It took her a second to realise he meant me.

'I don't *want* to go to Becky's wedding,' I said.

I didn't want all the family looking at me, shaking their heads, whispering. I was sure they'd all compare me with the first Angela. I knew they'd say I wasn't a bit like her.

'There,' said Mum. 'That settles it.' But she looked doubtful.

She picked up her teacup but then put it down without a sip. The cup clattered in the saucer. It was obvious her hand was trembling.

'We'll all go,' Dad said firmly.

'Oh please, don't, both of you,' I said, getting up from the table. 'I'm going to school.'

I rushed off before I could get caught up in the argument. I tried to forget about it. I mucked around with Vicky and Sarah, I got told off for talking in class,

I got the giggles in singing, I played the fool on the hockey pitch doing a sword dance with my hockey stick, I wrote a very rude but very funny joke on the toilet wall – while Angela hovered above my head, her wings creating a cold breeze.

I didn't get the bus home with Vicky and Sarah. I walked right through the town and out to the cemetery instead. I don't know why.

Maybe I want to talk to Angela. And yet here I am assaulting her, slapping her stone angel around.

'I'm sorry,' I whisper, and I reach out and hold the angel's hand. Her fist stays clenched. She wouldn't want to hold hands with me. The bad sister.

I'm very late home. Mum is at the window, white-faced. She's already phoned Dad and he's come rushing home from work.

'Where have you *been?*' Mum says, bursting into tears.

'How could you be so thoughtless?' says Dad.

Mum can't ever bear me being ten minutes late because she's so scared there will have been another accident.

'I'm sorry, I'm sorry, I'm *sorry*,' I gabble. 'Look, I went to the cemetery, okay?'

'Oh, darling,' says Mum. She gives me a hug. Even Dad looks sheepish.

I feel guiltier than ever. They think I'm so devoted to my dead sister. They have no idea I sometimes can't stand her.

'Let's have tea,' says Mum.

'What's happening about Becky's wedding?'

'We needn't go. I'll write a note to explain – and we'll send her a nice present,' says Dad.

'Well. Maybe we *should* go. I think I was being a bit . . . selfish,' says Mum. 'We should wish Becky well. Angela – you know, *Angela* – she'd have wanted to go, wouldn't she? And it's right, we have this Angela, *our* Angela, to think of.'

'But I said. I don't want to go.'

It doesn't matter what I say. We're going. And that's that. Dad phones his sister. Mum writes an acceptance note. Dad buys a crystal decanter and glasses as a wedding gift. Mum chooses a new suit, blue with a black trim.

'You'll have to have a suit too, Angela.'

'*Me*?' When I'm out of school uniform I live in jeans and T-shirts.

'Come on now, Angela, use your head,' Mum says impatiently. 'You can't go to a wedding in trousers and trainers.'

She drags me all round this grim department store looking at the most terrible outfits. I moan and complain. Eventually we fetch up in Top Shop and I get a dress and a purple jacket and new shoes. I get quite excited at the way I look. Older, for a start, and although the shoes pinch like hell it's really cool to be wearing sexy high heels.

'You look lovely, Angela,' says Dad, when I dress up for him. I *feel* lovely too.

Not on the wedding day though. My hair won't go right for a start. It sticks out in a terrible frizz and won't be subdued. I've got little spots on my forehead and chin and I slap on so much make-up to cover them it looks like I'm wearing a beige mask. I have to wash and start all over again. I splash water on my dress and I'm scared it will mark. I'm not sure it really goes with the jacket now. My shoes are still beautiful, but whenever I try to walk I turn my ankle.

I'm going to look a right sight at the wedding. I stare at myself in the mirror. The first Angela peeps over my shoulder, her fine eyebrows raised.

Mum's having second thoughts too. When we set off her eyes are red and her nose is shiny and she clutches her lace hankie as if it's a cuddle blanket. Dad puts his arm round her and gives her a quick squeeze.

Everyone stares at us when we get to the church. People hang back as if our stale mourning is contagious – but then my aunt gives my dad a hug and soon everyone's whispering and waving and Mum manages to smile bravely and wave back. I keep my head down, glancing up under my fringe every now and then at all these relations who are practically strangers. I haven't got a clue who half the people are.

There's a good-looking lanky guy with dark hair who

peers round at me curiously. He's wearing a shirt the exact royal purple of my jacket. He grins, acknowledging this, I grin back foolishly. And then the organ music starts up and Becky and my uncle start down the aisle.

The dark guy keeps looking at me during the ceremony and the wedding breakfast. (Definitely *not* egg and bacon – and I'm allowed my very first glass of champagne.)

He doesn't come and talk until the disco starts. He stands behind my chair, fingering the jacket I've slung over the back.

'Snap,' he says.

'Snap.'

'Would you like to dance?'

Would I! Though the glass of champagne and my new high heels make me walk very warily onto the dance floor. He is really gorgeous – and he's asked *me* to dance. He's quite a bit older than me too, probably nineteen or twenty. A student. Smiling at me. I hope he doesn't know I'm only fourteen. I don't think he's family.

'What's your name?' I mumble shyly.

'James. And you're Angela.'

'How do you know?'

'Well. I live next door to Becky. I knew your sister.'

I miss a beat.

'You're not a bit like her,' he says.

I knew it.

'Not that I remember her all that well. I was only a little kid when she . . . But I remember that last summer because she came to stay with Becky. She had all this pretty blonde hair and big blue eyes, yes?'

'Like a little angel,' I say. I've stopped dancing.

'Mmm,' says James. He pauses. 'Well. Not exactly *angelic*. I was terrified of her, actually.'

'You were . . . what?'

'I was this pathetic little wimp, scared stiff of the big girls. They teased me and I blubbed and that only made them worse.'

'My sister Angela?'

'Becky wasn't too bad, but Angela gave the most terrible Chinese burns. And she had this way of pulling my ears, really twisting them. You're not into ear-twisting, are you?'

I shake my head, still too surprised to joke.

'So Angela really gave you a hard time? I just can't imagine her doing stuff like that.'

'No one else could either. Whenever I told on her she batted those blue eyes and looked so sweet and innocent that no one believed me. I'm sorry. Maybe I shouldn't talk about her like that.'

'No, no – tell me more,' I say, picking up the beat and dancing.

Up above, sparkling in the strobe lighting, Angela is taking off her halo, folding her feathery wings, little horns sprouting through her blonde curls. She's waving her new forked tail at me. My bad sister.

Other authors in the series

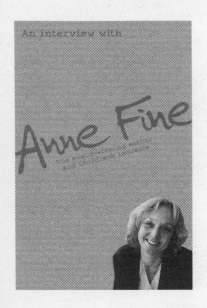

An interview with

Anne Fine

the sun-kissing author
and Children's Laureate

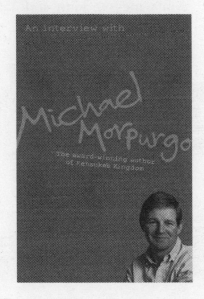

An interview with

Michael Morpurgo

The award-winning author
of Kensuke's Kingdom

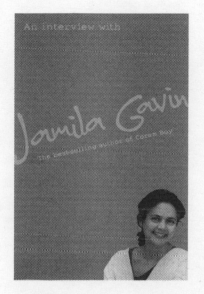

An interview with

Jamila Gavin

The bestselling author of Coram Boy

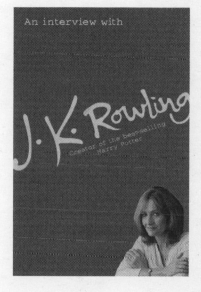

An interview with

J. K. Rowling

Creator of the bestselling
Harry Potter